GREECE

Written and photographed by
Julia Waterlow

Our Country

Australia
Canada
China
France
Greece
India
Italy
Japan
New Zealand
Pakistan
The Soviet Union
Spain
The United Kingdom
The United States
West Germany

Cover *An old monastery in the beautiful Greek countryside.*

Editor: Joanna Housley
Designer: David Armitage

First published in 1991 by
Wayland (Publishers) Ltd
61 Western Road, Hove
East Sussex BN3 1JD, England

British Library Cataloguing in Publication Data
Waterlow, Julia
  Greece. – (Our country)
  I. Title II. Series
  914.95

ISBN 1 85210 970 X

Typeset by Dorchester Typesetting Group Ltd
Printed in Italy by Rotolito Lombarda S.p.A.
Bound in France by A.G.M.

All words printed in **bold** are explained in the glossary on page 30.

Contents

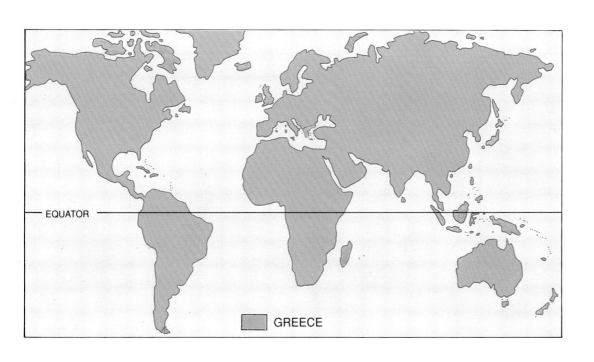

EQUATOR

GREECE

We live in Greece

Many tourists visit the famous ancient ruins at Delphi.

Greece is a country of mountains and islands, in the south east of Europe. About three-quarters of the land is covered in mountains and there are more than one thousand islands. Crete is the largest of these.

Greece has an **ancient** and great history. Old **temples**, **theatres** and other ruins can be seen in many parts of the country. **Tourists** come to visit these and to enjoy the sun and sea.

Today about ten million people live in Greece. About a third of them live in Athens, the capital city.

In this book, twelve children from all over Greece will tell you what it is like where they live.

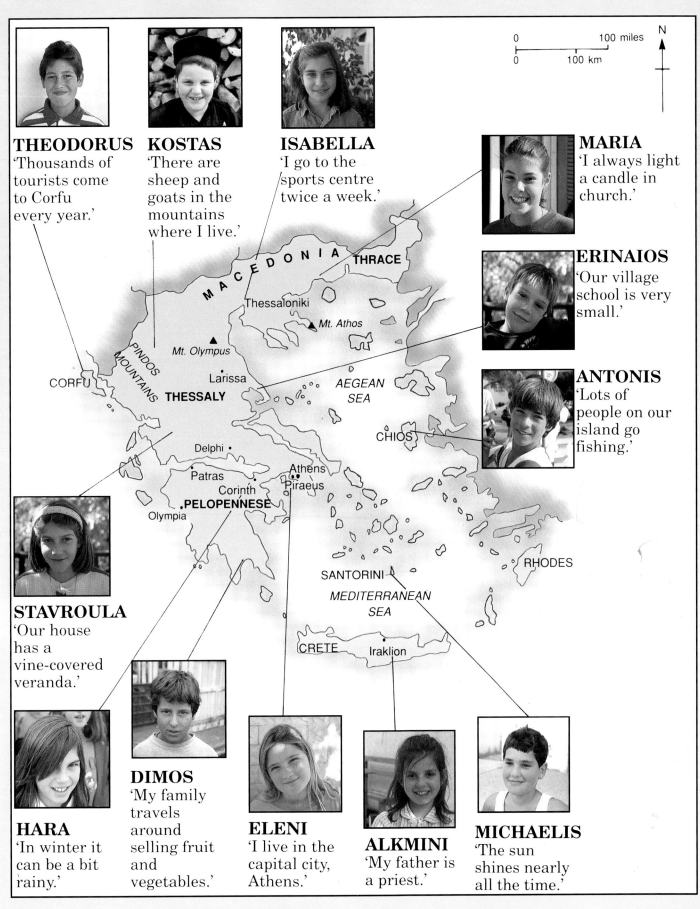

THEODORUS
'Thousands of tourists come to Corfu every year.'

KOSTAS
'There are sheep and goats in the mountains where I live.'

ISABELLA
'I go to the sports centre twice a week.'

MARIA
'I always light a candle in church.'

ERINAIOS
'Our village school is very small.'

ANTONIS
'Lots of people on our island go fishing.'

STAVROULA
'Our house has a vine-covered veranda.'

HARA
'In winter it can be a bit rainy.'

DIMOS
'My family travels around selling fruit and vegetables.'

ELENI
'I live in the capital city, Athens.'

ALKMINI
'My father is a priest.'

MICHAELIS
'The sun shines nearly all the time.'

0   100 miles
0   100 km

N

MACEDONIA   THRACE

Thessaloniki

Mt. Athos

PINDOS MOUNTAINS

Mt. Olympus

CORFU

Larissa

THESSALY

AEGEAN SEA

CHIOS

Delphi

Patras   Athens
Corinth   Piraeus

PELOPENNESE

Olympia

RHODES

SANTORINI

MEDITERRANEAN SEA

CRETE   Iraklion

The weather

Greece has hot summers and mostly mild winters. In the north and in the mountains it is quite cold all year round. Mountains like Mount Olympus, which is the highest at 2,917 m, have cold winters with plenty of snow for skiing. As well as being hot, summers are also sunny and dry, which makes Greece a popular place for tourists on their summer holidays.

The beautiful Pindos Mountains have snow on them in winter.

Sometimes there is little rain for months on end. Most rain falls in the winter, between November and March. The north and the mountains in central Greece are usually a little wetter than other areas.

'It's getting cold now that winter is coming.'

'My name is Hara. Here I am with my friends. We've come on an outing to the **Acropolis** in Athens. In summer it's very hot and sunny here, but now it's November and it's getting colder. It's cloudy so I hope it doesn't rain – last week it poured down!'

'Even early in the morning it's hot in summer.'

'I am Antonis and I live on an island in the Aegean Sea. We have long, hot summers when it hardly ever rains. The fishing boats go out every night and bring in fish early in the morning. In summer it's already very hot when they come back.'

A dry wind, called the *meltemi,* blows for much of the summer from the north across the Aegean Sea. This can make the journeys from island to island by boat very rough.

Farming

The richest farming areas in Greece are the **plains** on the mainland: Thessaly, Macedonia and Thrace. Here the main **crops** are cotton, **cereals** and tobacco. Fruit and nuts grow in many places. As well as apples and grapes, it is warm enough for fruit like oranges and lemons.

Much of Greece is too hilly and the soil too poor for crops like these. Instead, olive trees are grown because they do well even on the poorest land. In the hills there are big flocks of sheep and goats. Many of the people living on the islands and by the sea are fishermen.

In early winter farmers collect olives from the olive trees.

'My family makes wine from the grapes.'

'My name is Alkmini. Like many people in the area where we live, my family grows grapes. Here my father and brother are putting the grapes into a machine called a press which squashes them so the juice comes out. They will make wine with the grape juice.'

'We keep sheep in the mountains.'

'I am Kostas and here I am with my father's sheep. Lots of people in our mountain village own sheep or goats. Every day the shepherds go out and take the animals out to **graze** on the hillsides. The leading goats or sheep have bells on and from a distance it sounds like someone is playing a tune.'

Most farms are small and family-owned. Children often help their parents when they are not at school. Although farmers do use tractors, many still use animals, such as mules, to do the heavy work.

9

Industry and jobs

Shipping is an important industry. There are many ports in Greece.

One of the biggest industries in Greece is tourism. About nine million tourists visit every year – nearly as many as the whole Greek **population**! A lot of island people now live from the money the tourists spend.

Many Greek industries use the crops grown on farms, like cotton to make clothes, tobacco to make cigarettes, and olives to make olive-oil. Another big industry is making cement.

Most factories are based near Athens, or Thessaloniki in the north. Piraeus, near Athens, is Greece's biggest port. It is famous for its shipping industry.

Greeks like to own their own businesses and there are many small shops and companies. Most people work in the morning, rest in the afternoon when it is hottest, and start work again in the early evening.

'Look at our lorry and see all the boxes!'

'I am Dimos and my family owns this lorry. My parents buy fruit and vegetables from the farms and then we come to the market to sell them. We travel around a lot. At the moment we are living in our tent outside a town called Kalamata. There are many other travellers here too.'

'My mother owns this tourist shop.'

'My name is Theodorus. I live on the island of Corfu, which thousands of tourists visit every year. This is my mother's shop. She sells silver jewellery, hand-made rugs, pottery and **icons**, which are religious paintings. She says the Italian tourists buy the most icons and the Germans like the jewellery.'

Schools

Most children go to school from 8.30 am to 1.30 pm five days a week. They go home for lunch. Many have extra private lessons, paid for by their parents, in the afternoon or evening. Music, dancing, sports and languages are popular private classes because schools do not always teach these subjects.

From ages six to twelve children go to primary school, and then gymnasium (secondary school) until they are fifteen. Some then go to **lyceum** for another three years before going on to university. The general subjects at school are maths, geography, Greek and religion. Children also have many lessons about Greek history.

A classroom at a village school.

Schools are free for everyone but they are often crowded. In some villages there is only one classroom for all the different-aged children.

'Every day I have private lessons after school.'

'I am Maria. Every Tuesday afternoon I have private piano lessons. I come back from school at 1.30 pm, eat my lunch and then go for a piano lesson. After piano lessons I have either maths or language lessons. I also have to do lots of homework for school!'

'I go to the local village school.'

'My name is Erinaios. Here I am at my local village school. There is just one classroom and one teacher for all twenty of us. The youngest pupil is six and the oldest is twelve. Our teacher has given me some exercises to do on my own while he is teaching the older children.'

Religion

There are small churches like this all over Greece.

Almost everyone in Greece belongs to the Greek Orthodox Church. This is part of the **Christian** religion. On Sundays many people go to services in their local church.

Every town and village has a church. Even in the countryside there are small churches scattered among the fields. Greece also has **monasteries**, usually built in quiet places. Mount Athos is a famous group of monasteries that does not allow women or children to visit.

The **priests** in Greece wear black robes with tall black hats. They are not supposed to shave or cut their hair. Many have long

14

'My father is the village priest.'

'My name is Alkmini and this is my father. He is the village priest. He has just come back from the church. When he holds a service in church he puts on gold and white robes instead of his everyday black ones. He is also a farmer. He just wears ordinary clothes when he's working on the farm.'

'When I go to church I kiss the icons.'

'My name is Maria. I'm named after the Virgin Mary. Many Greek children are named after saints. Here I am kissing an icon. I always kiss the icons and light a candle when I go to church. I put a few drachma in a box to help the church.'

beards and tie their hair in a bun at the back of their heads. Churches have icons (religious pictures) but no statues. Icons are often found in people's homes and in shops, buses and taxis.

Festivals

Most festivals in Greece are religious. The biggest in the year is Easter. There are **carnivals** before Easter, and on Easter Day bells ring out and fireworks shoot into the sky. A special feast follows. Eggs are painted red and piled in a bowl on the table. The main part of the meal is usually lamb, often roasted over an open fire.

Churches have their own festivals, with services followed by music and dancing. Every child, too, has a celebration on the day of the saint they are named after, called their 'name day'. It is like a birthday.

The religious festival of St Spiridon on Corfu.

Friends come to visit and bring cakes or small presents.

Christmas, St Basil's Day (the first day of the New Year) and public holidays are celebrated too.

'Today is my friend's birthday.'

'I am Isabella and I'm wearing my favourite party dress with flowers on it. Today it's my friend's birthday. Can you see how old she is by the number of candles on her birthday cake? As well as our birthdays we also celebrate the day of the saint we are named after. It's like having two birthdays!'

'On festival days I wear these special clothes.'

'I am Kostas. My family are people from the Pindos Mountains known as *Vlachs*. We are very proud of our history and on special festival days I wear these traditional clothes. Last time I wore them was for the Independence Day parade on 25th March. Look at the pompoms on my shoes!'

Homes

White houses on the island of Santorini.

All over Greece houses and flats have terraces, verandas, or balconies so people can sit outside. Often these are covered with **vines** to shade them from the hot summer sun. Usually there are lots of pot plants on the balconies and the flowers make the houses look very colourful. People spend a lot of time outside because the weather is so warm and sunny.

Athens is crowded with blocks of flats where city people live. In the country most families have a house. In the hills houses are often built of stone. On the islands and in the south houses are often painted white, which helps reflect the sun and keeps the rooms cool.

18

'Our house has a vine-covered veranda.'

'I am Stavroula. I'm sitting on the veranda of our house doing some embroidery. It's hot in the sun but our veranda is shaded by a vine which grows over it. Mum grows all sorts of plants in the red pots behind me. Mostly she grows flowers but some of the pots have herbs in them.'

'We use the sun to heat our water.'

'I am Michaelis and here I am on the roof of our house with my sister. I am standing next to a 'solar panel'. It has water inside it which heats up in the sun and is stored in the tank above. It's nearly always sunny on our island, so the sun gives us hot water whenever we want it!'

Family life is important. Those who work away from home, often in Athens, always return to the family for holidays and festivals.

Sport and pastimes

The famous Olympic Games began at Olympia in Greece in 776 BC. The first modern Olympic Games were held in Athens in 1896 and now take place in different countries every four years.

Popular sports in Greece are football, volleyball and basketball. The sea is never far away, so many people go to the beach at weekends for swimming and fishing. In winter, some go skiing in the mountains.

Backgammon is a popular board game in Greece.

Greek people enjoy talking, and meet in cafés to drink coffee and to chat. On warm Sunday evenings families take a stroll in the main street of their town or village, stopping to talk to their friends. Most families have a television at home and many young people like to go to the cinema.

'I like playing football in the village square.'

'I am Erinaios. Here I am beside the fountain in the *platia*, the village square. The village I live in is in the hills and there isn't much flat ground to play sports on. But the *platia* is great for football. And when I'm thirsty I can have a drink from the fountain!'

'I go running at the sports centre.'

'My name is Isabella. On Saturday mornings I go to the sports centre with my friend. She's the one with blonde hair. We're about to have a race. Our teacher always makes us do warming up exercises before we start running.'

Food

Stuffed vegetables like these tomatoes and courgettes make a popular meal in Greece.

Breakfast in Greece is often just a cup of coffee. Later in the morning people eat a snack like a *tiropita*, which is a tasty cheese pie. Lunch is around 2.00 pm, after school or work has finished. Supper is sometimes late in the evening.

Salads are often served with the meal, as well as *feta* cheese (made from sheep or goat's milk) and olives. Bread is always put on the table. The main dish might be some kind of stuffed vegetable or fresh fish or grilled meat. *Souflaki*, which are chunks of lamb or pork on a **skewer**, are often bought at street corners for snacks. Olive-oil and herbs are used in all the dishes.

'We have bread with every meal.'

'My name is Kostas. Mum sent me to buy the bread to go with the bean soup she's cooking for our lunch. We have bread with every meal. At the bakery I wanted to buy a *baklava* (that's a cake made with honey and nuts) but Mum wouldn't give me the money for it until I'd done my homework!'

'We eat lunch when we get home from school.'

'I am Erinaios. Here I am eating outside our house with my friend. We have lunch when we get home from school. Today it's peppers stuffed with a mixture of rice, herbs and nuts. We have *feta* cheese and olives with the meal. Sometimes we just have a salad and bread, and I like yoghurt with honey afterwards.'

Usually Greeks finish a meal with fresh fruit or creamy yoghurt. They also love to eat sticky sweet cakes.

Shopping

Although there are some supermarkets, Greeks still prefer to buy their food in small shops and markets. There is always a baker's shop nearby where people go every day for their bread, cakes or pies. Usually they do the other food shopping once or twice a week.

In many places greengrocers drive around in open-backed vans, selling fresh fruit and vegetables. The driver calls out what he is selling, sometimes using a loudspeaker. The best place to buy fresh fish is at the harbour when the fishermen come to shore with their catch.

Many different kinds of olives are sold at this shop in the market.

'The kiosk sells sweets, crisps and drinks.'

'I am Theodorus. I'm going to buy a bag of crisps at the kiosk. There are lots of kiosks in Corfu town but this one is close to my Mum's shop, where I come every day after school. When it's hot in summer, I often buy an ice-cream or a cold drink here.'

'Things are usually cheaper at the market.'

'My name is Maria and I am buying flowers at the Saturday market. Many of the stalls have umbrellas over them because it can be so hot in the sun. People come from outside town in vans and trucks to sell fruit, vegetables, fish, clothes and household things like plates and bowls.'

Every town and village has little **kiosks** selling magazines, sweets, pens and other useful everyday things. In Athens there are large fashion stores, but most Greek shops are small, family-run businesses.

Transport

With so many islands, boats and ferries are one of the most important ways of getting around, both for local people and for tourists. These ferries can take cars, lorries and buses as well as people. On the mainland many families have a car. The islands do not all have roads and people may walk or ride bicycles or mules.

Buses serve most towns and villages, though some small places have a bus only once or twice a week. In the countryside, particularly in the hills where the villages have steep narrow streets, mules and donkeys are still used for transport.

A passenger ferry arrives at an island harbour.

Greece has fewer railways than other European countries because the land is so mountainous. There are airports all over Greece, especially at the popular tourist places.

'You need a ticket before you get on the bus.'

'I am Eleni. I live in Athens and here I am on a city bus. Lots of people travel by bus. You need tickets before you get on – you can buy them at a kiosk. When you're on the bus you put a ticket in this machine next to me which stamps it.'

'Farmers use donkeys and mules in our village.'

'I am Michaelis. In my village on the island of Santorini some people still use donkeys and mules. Many streets are too narrow for cars. These donkeys are being used by farmers to carry things. They ride them too. I've never ridden one because I walk or bicycle wherever I want to go.'

Let's discuss Greece

Now you have read a little about Greece and the people, do you think their life is very different from yours? For example, look at what Maria and Erinaios say about school or Stavroula and Michaelis say about their homes. Is it like this where you live?

Greece is very popular with tourists. Why do you think people go on holiday to Greece? Would you like to go there?

Antonis said there were fishermen on his island. It is now difficult for them to make a good living because of **over-fishing** in the Mediterranean Sea. What other countries do you know by the Mediterranean Sea?

> **Facts**
>
> **Population:** 10 million
> **Capital:** Athens
> **Language:** Greek
> **Money:** Drachma
> **Religion:** Greek Orthodox

The famous view of the Acropolis in Athens.

Fishermen check their nets carefully when they come back from sea.

Isabella and Erinaios talked about the sports they play. Do you play the same sports? Find out some of the sports at the Olympic Games. Ask someone where and when the next Games are going to be held.

Tourists enjoy the sun, sand and sea on a Greek island.

Glossary

Acropolis A hill in Athens on which an ancient temple called the Parthenon stands.

Ancient Very old.

Carnivals Festivals with fairs and feasts.

Cereals Plants like wheat, barley, oats and maize.

Christianity The religion based on the teachings of Jesus Christ.

Crops Plants grown by farmers.

Graze To feed on growing grass.

Icon A picture of Jesus Christ, the Virgin Mary, or a saint.

Kiosks Open-sided small shops on the pavement.

Lyceum The Greek name for a higher secondary school.

Monasteries Places where monks live and pray.

Over-fishing Catching too many fish so there are not enough for the future.

Plains Large areas of flat land.

Population The number of people who live in a country.

Priest A person who leads religious services.

Skewer A metal or wooden stick used to hold pieces of food together.

Temples Buildings where people pray to their gods.

Theatres In Greece, places in the open air where people used to watch plays and other shows.

Tourists People who visit a country on holiday.

Vines The plants that grapes grow on.

Picture acknowledgements

All photographs by Julia Waterlow. Maps on contents page and page 5 by Jenny Hughes.

Books to read

Aglaia Lives in Greece by George Papapavlou (Young Library, 1984)

Alexander the Great and the Greeks by Nathaniel Harris (Wayland, 1985)

Children of the World, Greece (Gareth Stevens Children's Books, 1989)

Countries of the World, Greece by Peggy Hollinger (Wayland, 1989)

Find out about Ancient Greeks by Casey Horton (Hamish Hamilton, 1985)

Focus on Greece by Brian Dicks (Hamish Hamilton, 1988)

Greek Food and Drink by Irene Tavlarios (Wayland, 1987)

I am a Greek Orthodox by Maria Roussou (Franklin Watts, 1985)

Legends of Ancient Greece by Karin Sisti (Hamlyn, 1983)

People and Places, Greece by Bridget and Neil Ardley (Macmillan, 1989)

Index